D0012177

THE POCKET
AUSSIE
FACT BOOK

Other books in the Penguin Pocket Series

THE AUSTRALIAN CALORIE COUNTER
THE AUSTRALIAN EASY SPELLER
AUSTRALIAN GARDENING CALENDAR
CASSEROLES FOR FAMILY AND FRIENDS
CHAIRING AND RUNNING MEETINGS
CHESS MADE EASY
CHOOSING A NAME FOR YOUR BABY
CHOOSING AUSTRALIAN WINES
THE COMPACT GUIDE TO WRITING LETTERS
FAMILY FIRST AID
GABRIEL GATÉ'S FAST PASTA
GABRIEL GATÉ'S FAVOURITE FAST RECIPES
GABRIEL GATÉ'S ONE-DISH DINNERS
GOOD FOOD FOR BABIES AND TODDLERS
HOW TO MAKE OVER 200 COCKTAILS
HOW TO PLAY MAH JONG
HOW TO SELL ANYTHING BY SOMEONE WHO HAS
JULIE STAFFORD'S FAT, FIBRE AND ENERGY COUNTER
JULIE STAFFORD'S JUICING BOOK
MICROWAVE MEALS IN MINUTES
MICROWAVE TIPS AND TECHNIQUES
THE PENGUIN BOOK OF ETIQUETTE
THE PENGUIN POCKET BOOK OF QUOTATIONS
PLAYING CASINO GAMES TO WIN
THE POCKET CAKES AND PUDDINGS COOKBOOK
THE POCKET MUFFIN BOOK
THE POCKET SOUP COOKBOOK
THE POCKET WOK COOKBOOK
REMOVING STAINS
SPEAKING IN PUBLIC
TRAINING YOUR MEMORY
USING YOUR NOODLES
WEDDING ETIQUETTE
YOUR NEW BABY

THE POCKET
AUSSIE
FACT BOOK

MARGARET NICHOLSON

Penguin Books

Penguin Books

Published by the Penguin Group
Penguin Books Australia Ltd
250 Camberwell Road
Camberwell, Victoria 3124, Australia
Penguin Books Ltd
80 Strand, London WC2R 0RL, England
Penguin Putnam Inc.
375 Hudson Street, New York, New York 10014, USA
Penguin Books, a division of Pearson Canada
10 Alcorn Avenue, Toronto, Ontario, Canada, M4V 3B2
Penguin Books (N.Z.) Ltd
Cnr Rosedale and Airborne Roads, Albany, Auckland, New Zealand
Penguin Books (South Africa) (Pty) Ltd
24 Sturdee Avenue, Rosebank, Johannesburg 2196, South Africa
Penguin Books India (P) Ltd
11, Community Centre, Panchsheel Park, New Delhi 110 017, India

First published by Penguin Books Australia Ltd 1997
This third edition published 2002

10 9 8 7 6 5 4 3 2 1

Design by Brad Maxwell, Penguin Design Studio
Typeset in 9/12pt Stone Sans by Post Pre-press Group, Brisbane
Printed and bound in Australia by McPherson's Printing Group,
Maryborough, Victoria

National Library of Australia
Cataloguing-in-Publication data:

Nicholson, Margaret, 1931– .
 The pocket Aussie fact book.

 3rd ed.
 Bibliography.

 ISBN 0 14 300141 8.

 1. Australia – Miscellanea. I. Title.

994

www.penguin.com.au

Contents

Preface   vii

History   1
Australia Overview   17
   Location   17
   Area   17
   Distances   18
   Landform   19
   Climate   19
   Time zones   19
   Population   22
   Flags   23
   Coat of arms   24
   Emblems   24
   Anthems   24

   Public holidays &
      special days   26
Government   28
Economy   36
Currency   46
State by State   49
   Australian Capital
      Territory   49
   New South Wales   52
   Victoria   56
   Queensland   60
   South Australia   64
   Western Australia   68
   Tasmania   72
   Northern Territory   76

Famous Australians 80
   Architects 80
   Aviators 80
   Businesspeople 81
   Cartoonists 81
   Engineers &
     inventors 82
   Scientists &
     medicos 82
   Literature 82
   Theatre 84
   Radio 84
   Television 85
   Film 85
   Contemporary
     music 87
   Rock Bands 89
   Classical music 90
   Ballet & dance 90
   Opera 91
   Art 92
   Major Australian Films
     1970–2002 93

Sporting Greats 96
   Tennis 96
   Cricket 98
   Golf 100
   Swimming 102
   AFL 105
   NRL 106
   Rugby Union 107
   Soccer 108
   Boxing 109
   Melbourne Cup 110
Fauna 112
   Mammals 112
   Reptiles &
     amphibians 115
   Insects 116
   Arachnids 117
   Marine organisms 117
   Birds 118
Flora 122

Acknowledgements 125
List of Sources 126

Preface

Most people are interested in knowing what makes a country 'tick'. Most are not greatly concerned with the past but are vitally aware of forces shaping their lives today. However, to discover these forces it is necessary to look back at events in our history and to people who have helped mould them – people who, at the time, had little knowledge that they were part of the grand plan which has shaped our nation.

I have always considered myself fortunate to be an Australian. I think Australia is one of the most wonderful places on earth. Researching Australian facts gives me great pleasure and I hope that this little book may help you understand more about what makes this country so exciting.

History

The Australian Aborigines existed in almost total isolation for over 60 000 years. They had no written history, but investigation of Dreamtime stories, cave paintings and etchings reveals a culture remarkable in its complexity and richness. Strong spiritual ties link them to the land which influences their lives from birth to death. Each person embraces a plant or animal 'totem' with specific rules of behaviour.

Before white settlement, more than 600 tribes based their lives on hunting, fishing and seed gathering. Evidence suggests that ground-edged tools were used by Aborigines 10 000 years before they were used in Europe.

The colonisation of the land from 1788 by white settlers almost destroyed this fragile society. Many Aborigines were separated from their spiritual home and became dispossessed.

In 1850 segregation laws were passed to protect the Aborigines from poverty by confining them to missions or reserves, on the fringe of white society. Problems in health, housing and education became endemic.

In the 1950s attitudes began to change. Aborigines became more aware of their identity and white society recognised the appalling treatment they had suffered. Health services were overhauled and housing and education services became a national priority. Even so, in 2002 enormous problems still remain.

Aborigines were granted the vote in 1962 and were included in the census for the first time in 1967. It was not until 1992, when the High Court of Australia handed down the landmark *Mabo* judgement, that Aborigines who could prove unbroken occupancy of land could lodge a claim to that land. Then followed the *Wik* decision of 1996, which held that the grant of pastoral leases did not necessarily extinguish native title and that in some circumstances the two could coexist. In 1998 the Federal Court of Australia ruled that native title can exist over coastal waters. In the *Yorta Yorta* native title claim the Federal Court ruled that, in some cases, 'the tide of history can wash away entitlement'.

Historical notes

'Terra Australis incognita' was inhabited by its Aboriginal people.

1606	Willem Jansz lands on the west coast of Cape York, Queensland.
1616	Dirk Hartog lands on the island later named after him, off the west coast of Australia.
1642	Abel Tasman discovers Van Diemen's Land (Tasmania).
1770	Captain James Cook lands at Botany Bay. He names the eastern coastline 'New South Wales' for Britain.
1788	Beginning of European settlement as a penal colony. Arrival of Governor Arthur Phillip and First Fleet at Botany Bay on 18 January, then at Port Jackson on 26 January. Phillip formally takes possession of the eastern part of the continent including Van Diemen's Land.
1793	First free settlers arrive.
1796	Discovery of coal at the mouth of the Hunter River (Newcastle), New South Wales.
1797	Introduction of merino sheep by John Macarthur.
1798	George Bass and Matthew Flinders circumnavigate Van Diemen's Land in the *Norfolk*.
1802	Discovery of Port Phillip (Victoria) and Port Bowen (Queensland) by Lieutenant John Murray. Matthew Flinders discovers St Vincent Gulf and Spencer Gulf, South Australia.
1804	Lieutenant David Collins establishes a settlement on the lower Derwent River, Van Diemen's Land.

1807	First shipment of saleable wool to England.
1808	The Rum Rebellion. Deposition of Governor William Bligh.
1813	Crossing of Blue Mountains by Gregory Blaxland, William Charles Wentworth and William Lawson.
1814	Matthew Flinders suggests the name 'Australia' instead of New Holland.
1817	The first bank, Bank of New South Wales (now Westpac), is established.
1819	Lieutenant Phillip King discovers Port Essington, Northern Territory.
1822	Establishment of penal settlement at Macquarie Harbour, Van Diemen's Land.
1823	Brisbane River discovered by John Oxley and three convicts.
1825	Separation of the administration of Van Diemen's Land from New South Wales. Establishment of settlement at Brisbane.
1828	First census taken: 36 000 convicts and free settlers, 2549 military personnel; Aborigines not counted.
1829	First settlement at Swan River, Western Australia. Perth founded.
1834	First settlement at Twofold Bay, New South Wales. Henty brothers form settlement at Portland (Victoria).

1835	Foundation of Melbourne planned by Sir Richard Bourke.
1836	Settlement at Adelaide under Governor Sir John Hindmarsh.
1838	Captain James Bremer establishes Port Essington, Northern Territory.
1839	Area around where Darwin now stands discovered by crew of the *Beagle*.
1840	Transportation of convicts to New South Wales abolished.
1841	New Zealand proclaimed a separate colony.
1842	First elected council in New South Wales.
1847	Melbourne proclaimed a city.
1850	Sydney University founded. Representative government granted to Port Phillip, Van Diemen's Land and South Australia.
1851	Gold discovered in New South Wales by Edward Hargraves. The Port Phillip district becomes a separate colony named 'Victoria'.
1852	Transportation of convicts to Van Diemen's Land and Norfolk Island abolished.
1854	Eureka Stockade riot at Ballarat (Victoria) sparked by gold-miners' objections to high mining licence fees.
1855	Van Diemen's Land renamed 'Tasmania' after its discoverer, Abel Tasman. Responsible government

granted to New South Wales, Victoria and Tasmania.

1856	Responsible government granted to South Australia.
1857	Adult males granted the right to vote in Victoria.
1858	Adult males granted the right to vote in New South Wales.
1859	Queensland proclaimed a separate colony.
1861	Explorers Burke and Wills die while trying to reach Gulf of Carpentaria.
1863	Northern Territory comes under the jurisdiction of South Australia. Gold discovered at Kalgoorlie, Western Australia.
1868	Last transport bringing convicts to Australia lands in Fremantle, Western Australia.
1869	Darwin becomes a permanent settlement.
1872	Transcontinental telegraph completed carrying the first cable message from Sydney to London.
1876	Death of Truganini, last full-blooded Tasmanian Aborigine.
1878	First telephone in Australia.
1880	Ned Kelly, bushranger and rebel, captured.
1883	Silver discovered at Broken Hill, New South Wales.
1885	Australians go to war for the first time as New South Wales contingent sent to Sudan, Africa. BHP company floated.

1890	John Forrest becomes Western Australia's first premier.
1899	Sir Henry Parkes delivers his 'Tenterfield Address' on federation.
1900	Australia announces its intention of becoming independent from Great Britain.
1901	The Commonwealth of Australia is proclaimed on 1 January. First federal election held. Census gives population as 3 773 801 whites. Aborigines were not counted.
1902	Women granted the right to vote in federal elections.
1908	Canberra chosen as site for national capital.
1910	First Commonwealth banknotes issued.
1911	Douglas Mawson leads expedition to Antarctic.
1913	First Commonwealth postage stamps issued.
1914	World War I declared and Australian and New Zealand Army Corps (ANZAC) formed.
1915	ANZAC troops land at Gallipoli on 25 April; evacuated 18 December.
1917	Completion of transcontinental railway.
1918	First wireless message from London to Sydney. Australia House in London opened by George V.
1919	Return of Australian troops from Europe. Aviators Ross and Keith Smith make the first flight from England to Australia.

1920	Queensland and Northern Territory Aerial Services (QANTAS) formed by Hudson Fysh. White population now 5 411 300.
1922	Queensland the first state to abolish the death penalty.
1923	Construction of Sydney Harbour Bridge commences.
1927	Seat of government moved from Melbourne to Canberra.
1928	Aviator Kingsford Smith flies from America to Australia in *Southern Cross*. Flying doctor service begins. First traffic lights installed in Melbourne.
1929	Beginning of Depression. Fall in exports. Commonwealth government mobilises gold reserves.
1932	Sydney Harbour Bridge opened. Lang government in New South Wales dismissed.
1935	Kingsford Smith lost without trace near the Bay of Bengal. Ansett Airways set up by Reginald Ansett.
1936	Hume Reservoir on the Murray River completed.
1940	20 000 Australian troops embark for service overseas in World War II. Introduction of food, petrol and clothing rationing.
1941	Sinking of HMAS *Sydney* and HMAS *Canberra*. Australian troops besieged at Tobruk.
1942	Darwin and Katherine bombed. Japanese midget submarines in Sydney Harbour.

1943	Industrial conscription introduced.
1944	Pay-as-you-earn (PAYE) taxation introduced. Japanese prisoners of war attempt mass break-out at Cowra, New South Wales – 234 killed.
1946	United Nations grants trusteeship of New Guinea to Australia.
1947	Commonwealth Arbitration Commission established. Immigration program begun.
1948	40-hour week introduced. General Motors–Holden produces first Holden car. Food and clothing rationing ends.
1949	The right to vote granted to some Aborigines. Snowy Mountains hydro-electric scheme commenced. Robert Menzies becomes Prime Minister (Liberal Party).
1950	Petrol rationing ends. Australian troops join UN forces in Korea.
1951	ANZUS Treaty signed by Australia, New Zealand and USA against aggression in the Pacific.
1952	Uranium discovered at Rum Jungle, Northern Territory.
1953	Atomic Energy Commission established. Television Bill passed. Atomic weapons tested by Great Britain at Woomera, South Australia. South-East Asia Treaty Organisation (SEATO) founded.
1954	Queen Elizabeth II makes the first visit to Australia

by a reigning monarch. Troops withdrawn from Korea. 'Petrov Affair': accusations of communist espionage in Department of External Affairs.

1956   Olympic Games held in Melbourne.

1958   The first nuclear reactor opened at Lucas Heights, Sydney.

1960   Aborigines were granted citizenship and therefore entitlement to social service benefits. Reserve Bank established.

1961   Huge iron-ore deposits found at Pilbara, Western Australia.

1962   Standard-gauge railway opened between Brisbane, Sydney and Melbourne. Aborigines granted the vote. USA granted permission to build communication base at Exmouth, Western Australia, and space tracking station at Tidbinbilla, near Canberra.

1964   HMAS *Voyager* collides with HMAS *Melbourne* – 82 die.

1965   Australian infantry battalion sent to Vietnam. Australia imposes economic sanctions against Rhodesia.

1966   Decimal currency introduced on 14 February. Aborigines appeal to the UN for human rights. Sir Robert Menzies retires as prime minister. Metric system of weights and measures phased in.

1967	Prime Minister Harold Holt disappears at Portsea, Victoria. Aborigines included in census for the first time. Ronald Ryan hanged, the last person to be hanged in Australia.
1968	First Australian heart transplant performed. John Gorton becomes leader of the Liberal Party and prime minister.
1969	HMAS *Melbourne* collides with USS *Frank E Evans* with the loss of 74 lives. Poseidon company announces a nickel discovery and share prices soar. Bob Hawke elected president of the Australian Council of Trade Unions (ACTU). Equal pay for work of equal value granted to women.
1970	Demonstrations against Australian and US involvement in Vietnam. Tullamarine Airport in Melbourne opened.
1971	Australia ends fighting role in Vietnam. Lake Pedder in Tasmania flooded as part of hydroelectric scheme.
1972	Australian Labor Party victory under Gough Whitlam. Troops withdrawn from Vietnam. Formal ending of White Australia immigration policy.
1973	18-year-olds allowed to vote in federal elections.
1974	Cyclone Tracy hits Darwin on Christmas Day. Bankcard introduced.
1975	Whitlam government dismissed by Governor-

General, Sir John Kerr. Liberal – Country Party coalition wins election under Malcolm Fraser. Papua New Guinea becomes independent. No-fault divorce introduced.

1978   Northern Territory becomes responsible for its own administration.

1979   Aboriginal Land Trust gains title to 144 properties formerly Aboriginal reserves.

1980   Baby Azaria Chamberlain allegedly taken by a dingo at Uluru (Ayers Rock).

1982   New South Wales introduces random breath testing of drivers. Lindy Chamberlain found guilty of the murder of her daughter, Azaria.

1983   Labor Party gain government under Bob Hawke. *Australia II* wins America's Cup.

1984   World's first test-tube quads born in Melbourne.

1985   Federal government allows the application for a banking licence from 16 foreign banks.

1986   Fringe benefits tax is introduced. Bombing of Russell Street police headquarters.

1987   Share market collapses. Seven people killed in the Hoddle Street massacre, Melbourne.

1988   Australia celebrates bicentenary of white settlement. Queen opens new Parliament House. Charges against Lindy Chamberlain and her husband, Michael, are quashed.

1989	Newcastle suffers devastating earthquake leaving twelve dead. Australian cricket team brings home the Ashes for the first time in 34 years.
1990	Corporate failures continue as worst recession for 40 years takes hold.
1991	Government bans mining of uranium at Coronation Hill, Kakadu. Heart transplant pioneer Dr Victor Chang murdered. Nine die in massacre in Strathfield Shopping Plaza. Paul Keating takes over from Bob Hawke as prime minister.
1992	Landmark Mabo High Court decision enables Aborigines with unbroken occupancy of land to claim title. Sydney Harbour tunnel opens.
1993	ALP wins record fifth successive term. Sydney wins the right to host the 2000 Olympics.
1994	Drought blankets eastern Australia. Bodies of seven murdered backpackers found in the Belanglo State Forest, NSW.
1995	Rugby Super League controversy rages. Balance of payments deficit high. John Howard takes over as Liberal Party leader.
1996	Landslide victory to Liberal Party. John Howard becomes prime minister. Massacre at Port Arthur in Tasmania, 35 dead. Gun Summit bans all automatic and some semi-automatic weapons. 18 soldiers die in Blackhawk helicopter crash in

Queensland. Backpacker murderer Ivan Milat convicted. Martin Bryant given 35 life sentences for the massacre at Port Arthur.

1997   Wood Royal Commission into corruption fore-shadows sweeping changes in NSW. BHP announces withdrawal of steel-making in New-castle. Four Australians dead after Maccabiah Games in Israel. Eighteen killed in Thredbo land-slide in NSW – Stuart Diver sole survivor.

1998   Four sailors perish in fire aboard HMAS *Westralia*. Two landmark Federal Court rulings that native title can exist over coastal waters, and that 'the tide of history can wash away entitlements' in native title claims. Five volunteers die in Victorian bushfires. Seven die in disastrous Sydney-to-Hobart Yacht Race.

1999   Salt Lake City Olympic bid scandal erupts, send-ing shock waves through AOC. Aboriginal embassy removed from the lawns of old Parlia-ment House after 15 years' residency. Australian troops lead Interfet peacekeeping forces in East Timor. BHP Newcastle closes after 84 years. Republic referendum results in a 'No' vote.

2000   Goods and Services Tax (GST) introduced. Fif-teen backpackers die in suspected arson attack in Childers, Queensland. Sydney Olympics an outstanding success.

2001   Sir Donald Bradman dies. Historic merger between BHP and Billiton (UK). Royal commission into HIH Insurance collapse. Australia's first legal injecting rooms approved. Australian Parliament celebrates its centenary. One.Tel collapses. *Tampa* incident highlights the issue of asylum seekers. Ansett airline collapses.

2002   Devastating bushfires in NSW inflict heavy toll on lives and property. Hunger strike by detained asylum seekers at Woomera. The 'children overboard' affair embroils the federal government in further controversy. Governor-General Peter Hollingworth under fire for inaction over his handling of child sex abuse allegations. Robert Paul Long convicted of the Childers backpacker murders. Alex Campbell dies and a state funeral is held for this last ANZAC. Sydney Airport sold for $5.6 billion. Unprecedented numbers of Australians killed and injured in bomb blast at nightclub in Bali.

Australia in its region

Australia Overview

Location
Australia consists of two land masses: mainland Australia and Tasmania. It lies on and extends south from the Tropic of Capricorn in the southern hemisphere between latitudes 10°41′ and 43°39′S and longitudes 113°9′ and 153°39′E. It is bounded by the Pacific Ocean to the east, the Indian Ocean to the west, the Arafura Sea to the north and the Southern Ocean to the south. The nearest neighbour is Papua New Guinea, 200 km north. Timor is 640 km to the north-west, New Zealand is 1920 km east, and Antarctica is 2000 km due south.

Area
The area of Australia is 7 682 300 square km. Australia is about the size of the mainland states of the United States, excluding Alaska, and approximately 24 times the size of the British Isles.

Distances

Mainland east–west, 3983 km; north–south, 3138 km. Coastline including Tasmania and off-shore islands, 36 735 km.

Landform

Australia is one of the oldest continents and, because of the effects of 250 million years of erosion, it has become the flattest land mass on earth. It is considered to be the most stable land mass in the world, being free of any major mountain-building events for the past 80 million years. But Australia has a wide variety of landforms – mostly consisting of vast ancient crystal blocks. The lowest elevation is Lake Eyre (South Australia), which is 16 metres below sea level, and the highest peak is Mt Kosciuszko, which is 2228 metres above sea level.

Climate

There are generally no great extremes of climate but it is varied because of the size of the continent. The temperature range is from 23–26°C north of the Tropic of Capricorn to 38–40°C in the north-west and arid plateaus and deserts of the interior. The southern areas are more temperate although subject to wide variations – high rainfall, extreme heat and irregular flooding and drought. Australia is considered to be one of the driest continents on earth.

Time zones

There are three time zones within the Australian continent. The eastern states – Queensland, New South Wales,

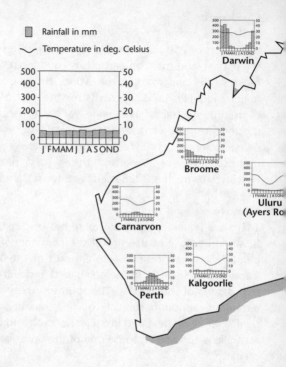

Rainfall in mm
Temperature in deg. Celsius

Darwin

Broome

Carnarvon

Uluru
(Ayers Ro

Perth

Kalgoorlie

20

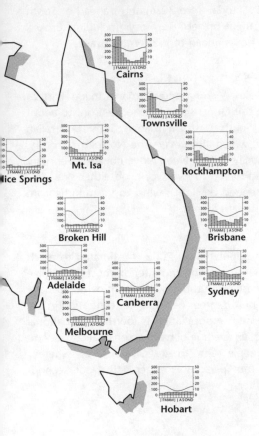

Cairns

Townsville

Mt. Isa

Rockhampton

lice Springs

Broken Hill

Brisbane

Adelaide

Canberra

Sydney

Melbourne

Hobart

Tasmania and Victoria – are 30 minutes ahead of South Australia and the Northern Territory (including Broken Hill), and two hours ahead of Western Australia.

Daylight saving

New South Wales, Victoria and Tasmania follow Eastern Summer Time but Queensland has decided not to adopt this practice. South Australia follows South Australian Summer Time, which also covers the Northern Territory. This period usually falls between November and February but can extend for up to two weeks on either side. Tasmania has extended daylight saving to six months from early October to late March.

Population
The Australian population in 2002 is estimated to reach 19.6 million. Because of the arid interior, most people live around the coastline. Although it is considered to have one of the highest degrees of urban concentration in the world, the density of population is low by international standards, with an average of two persons per square km. Many of its people came to Australia from elsewhere – one in every four persons is either a first- or second-generation settler.

Population distribution

Sydney	4 163 531	Adelaide	1 103 812
Melbourne	3 520 503	Canberra	315 272
Brisbane	1 659 586	Hobart	192 615
Perth	1 395 416	Darwin	91 324

Flags

From 1901 the Blue and Red Ensigns were generally regarded as official flags of the Commonwealth. In 1951 King George VI approved the recommendation  that the Blue Ensign become the official National Flag of Australia and the Red Ensign become the flag of the Australian merchant navy. The Blue Ensign is a plain blue flag with the Union Jack in the upper corner of the hoist, the seven-pointed Commonwealth star beneath and the five-starred Southern Cross to the right.

The state flags are based on the plain Blue Ensign with the particular badge of each state added. The Northern Territory flag is based on colours found in desert regions with the Territory's badge added.

Coat of arms

The present coat of arms was granted in 1912 by King George V. It consists of a shield composed of six parts, each containing one of the state badges. These  are surrounded by an ermine border, signifying the federation of the states into the Commonwealth. The shield is supported by two Australian animals, the kangaroo and the emu, standing on ornamental rests, behind which are small branches of wattle. The crest consists of the seven-pointed Commonwealth gold star, a symbol of national unity. At the base of the shield is a scroll on which is printed the word 'Australia'.

Emblems

The national floral emblem is the golden wattle and the national animal emblem is the kangaroo.

Anthems

The royal anthem, 'God Save the Queen', is used in the presence of Her Majesty the Queen or a member of the royal family.

The vice-regal salute which consists of the first four and last four bars of the national anthem, 'Advance Australia

Fair', is used in the presence of the governor-general.

The national anthem, 'Advance Australia Fair', is used on all other ceremonial occasions.

Advance Australia Fair

Australians all let us rejoice,
For we are young and free,
We've golden soil and wealth for toil;
Our home is girt by sea;
Our land abounds in nature's gifts
Of beauty rich and rare;
In history's page, let every stage
Advance Australia Fair.

Beneath our radiant Southern Cross,
We'll toil with hearts and hands;
To make this Commonwealth of ours
Renowned of all the lands;
For those who've come across the seas
We've boundless plains to share;
With courage let us all combine
To Advance Australia Fair.
In joyful strains then let us sing,
Advance Australia Fair.

Public holidays & special days

January	
1	New Year's Day
26	Australia Day

March	
first Monday	Labour Day (WA)
first Monday	8-hour Day (Tas)
second Monday	Labour Day (Vic)
third Monday	Canberra Day (ACT)

April	
first full moon	Easter (Good Friday to Easter Monday;
after equinox	Easter Tuesday holiday in some states)
(may fall in March)	
25	Anzac Day

May	
first Monday	Labour Day (Qld)
first Monday	May Day (NT)

June	
second Monday	Queen's Birthday (not WA)

August	
1	Wattle Day (some states)
first Monday	Bank Holiday (NSW)

September

1	Wattle Day (some states)

October

first Monday	Labour Day (NSW and ACT)
6	Queen's Birthday (WA)
second Monday	Labour Day (SA)

November

first Tuesday	Melbourne Cup Day (Melbourne metro only)
11	Remembrance Day

December

25	Christmas Day
26	Boxing Day (not SA)
28	Proclamation Day (SA)

Government

Australia's official name is the Commonwealth of Australia. Its form of government is a constitutional monarchy. The head of state is Queen Elizabeth II of the United Kingdom of Great Britain and Northern Ireland and also Queen of Australia. She is represented in Australia by the governor-general. The head of government is the prime minister, leader of the party or coalition of parties holding a majority in federal parliament.

Australia is an independent self-governing member of the British Commonwealth of Nations and a foundation member of the United Nations. It is in alliance with the United States of America and New Zealand in the ANZUS pact and a member of the South-East Asia Treaty Organisation (SEATO).

Australia is a federation of six states with two internal federal territories (Australian Capital Territory and Northern

Territory) and a number of external territories under its control – Norfolk Island, Cocos Island, Christmas Island, Lord Howe Island, Macquarie Island, and Australian Antarctica between longitudes 45° and 160°.

Federal government

The Australian federal parliament is based on the British Westminster system with a prime minister and cabinet. It is responsible for matters of national importance – defence, external affairs, customs and excise, communications, foreign trade, social services, treasury and immigration. It also shares mutual responsibilities with the state legislatures for education, agriculture, energy services, health and law enforcement.

There are two houses in the federal parliament – the House of Representatives (lower house) and the Senate (upper house).

House of Representatives

This is often called the people's house as the 150 members are voted in directly by the people of Australia with each member representing about 70 000 voters. The House consists of government and opposition members (MPs) voted in at the most recent general election. It sits for 70 to 80 days each year and is limited to a three-year period. However, it may be dissolved sooner by the governor-general on the advice of the prime minister. Its main function is to debate and discuss bills, which are proposed new laws. The debates within the House are regulated by the Speaker, who is chosen from among the governing party. The members sit on opposite sides of the House – the government to the right of the Speaker and the opposition to the left. Independents sit in the cross-benches facing the Speaker.

The Senate

This is virtually a house of review where the procedures are designed to allow debate on the merits or defects of any bill passed by the House of Representatives. The Senate can request amendments to, and can reject, any bill. In 2002 there were 76 senators, 12 from each state and 2 from each internal territory. Each senator represents the whole state, not just a small area. Senators from states are elected for a six-year period. Every three years half the senators retire but may stand for re-election. Senators from the territories are elected for three years.

The Ministry

This consists of members of the government who are responsible for a particular area of policy. Most ministers are members of the House of Representatives and a few are from the Senate. They have specific departments of the public service to help them administer their portfolios. The prime minister is, by convention, always a member of the House of Representatives. Ministers and other leading members of the government are called frontbenchers because they sit on the front benches in the parliament. Other members are called backbenchers.

The Opposition forms a shadow government with members in the same positions as the government.

Cabinet

This is an inner council and consists of the leading figures (those with senior portfolios) of the government and the Senate with the prime minister as chairman. Junior ministers attend cabinet meetings only when matters affecting their departments are being discussed.

The executive council

It advises the governor-general of major political decisions affecting the nation which have been made by the Cabinet.

The governor-general

He is the Queen's representative in the Australian parliament and is appointed by the Queen on the advice of the prime minister. All laws made by parliament finally depend on his assent. This should be a formality.

Prime ministers

Sir Edmund Barton	1 Jan 1901 – 24 Sep 1903
Alfred Deakin	24 Sep 1903 – 27 Apr 1904
John Christian Watson	27 Apr 1904 – 18 Aug 1904
George Reid	18 Aug 1904 – 5 Jul 1905
Alfred Deakin	5 Jul 1905 – 13 Nov 1908
Andrew Fisher	13 Nov 1908 – 2 Jun 1909
Alfred Deakin	2 Jun 1909 – 29 Apr 1910
Andrew Fisher	29 Apr 1910 – 24 Jun 1913
Sir Joseph Cook	24 Jun 1913 – 17 Sep 1914
Andrew Fisher	17 Sep 1914 – 27 Oct 1915
William Morris Hughes	27 Oct 1915 – 9 Feb 1922
Stanley Melbourne Bruce	9 Feb 1922 – 22 Oct 1929
James Henry Scullin	22 Oct 1929 – 6 Jan 1932
Joseph Aloysius Lyons	6 Jan 1932 – 7 Apr 1939
Sir Earle Page	7 Apr 1939 – 26 Apr 1939
Sir Robert Gordon Menzies	26 Apr 1939 – 29 Aug 1941
Sir Arthur W. Fadden	29 Aug 1941 – 7 Oct 1941
John Curtin	7 Oct 1941 – 5 Jul 1945
Francis Michael Forde	6 Jul 1945 – 13 Jul 1945
Joseph Benedict Chifley	13 Jul 1945 – 19 Dec 1949
Sir Robert Gordon Menzies	19 Dec 1949 – 26 Jan 1966
Harold Edward Holt	26 Jan 1966 – 19 Dec 1967
Sir John McEwen	19 Dec 1967 – 10 Jan 1968
Sir John Grey Gorton	10 Jan 1968 – 10 Mar 1971

Sir William McMahon	10 Mar 1971 – 8 Dec 1972
Edward Gough Whitlam	8 Dec 1972 – 11 Nov 1975
John Malcolm Fraser	11 Nov 1975 – 5 Mar 1983
Robert James Lee Hawke	5 Mar 1983 – 19 Dec 1991
Paul John Keating	19 Dec 1991 – 2 Mar 1996
John Winston Howard	2 Mar 1996 –

Voting

All Australian citizens over the age of 18 are eligible to vote. Voting is compulsory for everyone. Compulsory preferential voting is the most common system used in Australia. In voting for the House of Representatives one candidate only from any one party is selected to represent each electorate. The voter must vote for all the candidates in order of preference. If no candidate receives an absolute majority, then there is a distribution of preference votes.

The number of members of the House of Representatives depends on the population of each state. In 2002 there were 150 members, 50 for New South Wales, 37 for Victoria, 27 for Queensland, 12 for South Australia, 5 for Tasmania, 15 for Western Australia, 2 for the Australian Capital Territory and 2 for the Northern Territory.

Proportional representation is the other major electoral system in Australia. It is used in the Senate and in some state elections. Each senator represents a whole state; as the electorate is so large, more than one candidate is elected for each state. In 2002 there were 76 senators, 12 for each state and 2 for each territory.

State government

State governments run along the same lines as the federal government, each having a premier as leader, a cabinet and ministry, and an opposition. State parliaments deal with state affairs such as housing, trade, education, industry and law enforcement as well as sharing mutual responsibilities with the federal parliament.

Five states have both a lower house or Legislative Assembly (House of Assembly in South Australia and Tasmania) and an upper house or Legislative Council. Queensland opted to have only one house, a Legislative Assembly. The Northern Territory and Australian Capital Territory each have a Legislative Assembly.

Local government

The Local Government Act of 1919 gave power to areas as small as cities, municipalities and shires, to provide a more satisfactory system of government within the local area. The mayor or president is leader of a number of councillors who are elected by the residents of the area. The principal officer is a general manager who is responsible for the overall administration and is answerable to council. Directors or managers are in charge of various departments, such as health and development, planning, engineering and community affairs, and are answerable to the general manager. Australia has 900 bodies at local government level.

Judicial system

There are three types of courts at state level. Australia has 175 **local courts** (previously called Courts of Petty Sessions) which deal with 98% of all cases. They mostly deal with less serious offences and preliminary enquiries into major crimes. Parties can appeal to the **District (County) Court** where a judge hears civil cases and appeals. A judge and jury hear criminal cases and appeals. The **Supreme Court** has unlimited civil jurisdiction and hears the most serious criminal matters. Parties can appeal to the Federal Court of Australia and the High Court of Australia.

There are three federal courts. The **High Court** has jurisdiction over matters where the Commonwealth is a party. It also acts as a final court of appeal for cases from elsewhere in the system. The **Federal Court** deals with industrial matters, bankruptcy, trade practices and administrative review. The **Family Court** deals with marriage, divorce and custody and property settlement after a divorce.

Economy

The Australian economy follows the system of free enterprise and orderly marketing of products. In 1991 the tariff barrier was eased by the government.

The federal and state governments have separate areas of responsibility for raising and spending revenue. The financial year runs from 1 July to 30 June.

Federal government income

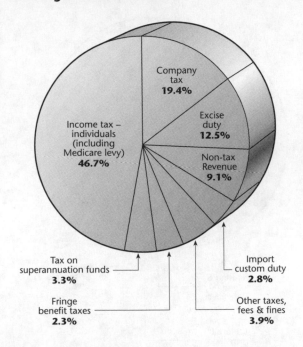

- Company tax **19.4%**
- Excise duty **12.5%**
- Income tax – individuals (including Medicare levy) **46.7%**
- Non-tax Revenue **9.1%**
- Tax on superannuation funds **3.3%**
- Fringe benefit taxes **2.3%**
- Import custom duty **2.8%**
- Other taxes, fees & fines **3.9%**

Federal government expenditure

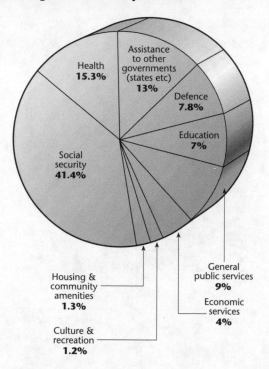

Health **15.3%**

Assistance to other governments (states etc) **13%**

Defence **7.8%**

Education **7%**

Social security **41.4%**

Housing & community amenities **1.3%**

Culture & recreation **1.2%**

General public services **9%**

Economic services **4%**

State government income

special Commonwealth government grants and payments	42%
tax revenue	41%
sales of goods and services	7%
other revenue	6%
financial distribution	4%

State government expenditure

public health	24.5%
education	23.5%
general public services	12.5%
law and order	11.0%
transport	9.5%
social security and welfare	7.5%
housing and community amenities	5%
culture and recreation	4%
agriculture, mining and forestry	2.5%

Trade

Australia trades with two main groups of countries: the European Union (EU), which consists of countries with common economic policies (such as France, Germany, Italy, Sweden and the UK); and the Asia–Pacific Economic Cooperation group (APEC), which includes Canada, USA, China, Japan, Indonesia, New Zealand, Singapore and Taiwan.

Imports

Australia imports mostly manufactured goods, machinery, transport equipment and chemicals totalling about $110.08 billion in the year 2000.

Exports

Australia exports mostly minerals, meat, cereals, textiles and manufactured goods totalling about $97.25 billion in the year 2000.

Overview of Australian industry

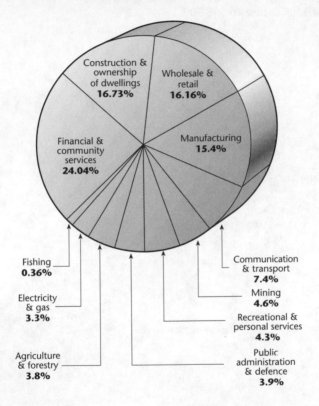

Construction & ownership of dwellings
16.73%

Wholesale & retail
16.16%

Manufacturing
15.4%

Financial & community services
24.04%

Fishing
0.36%

Electricity & gas
3.3%

Agriculture & forestry
3.8%

Communication & transport
7.4%

Mining
4.6%

Recreational & personal services
4.3%

Public administration & defence
3.9%

Australian agriculture 2001 (approx.)
Total cattle 26 598 000

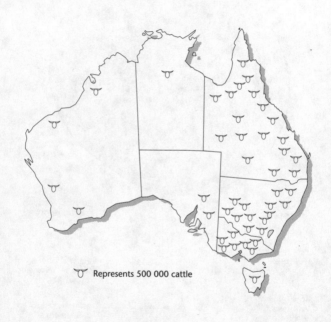

ʊ̈ Represents 500 000 cattle

Total sheep 115 456 000
Wool production 687 000 tonnes

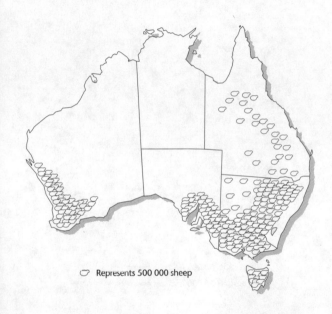

Represents 500 000 sheep

Total wheat 11 543 000 hectares; 21 456 000 tonnes
Coarse grain 4 875 000 hectares; 11 376 000 tonnes

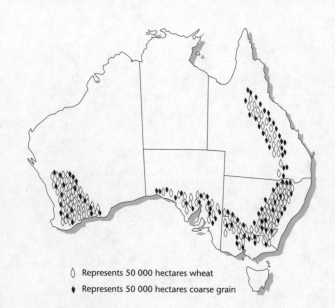

◊ Represents 50 000 hectares wheat

◆ Represents 50 000 hectares coarse grain

Sugar cane 402 000 hectares; 38 534 000 tonnes

Fruit and vines 268 265 hectares; 2 685 000 tonnes

Cotton 446 000 hectares; 1 547 000 tonnes

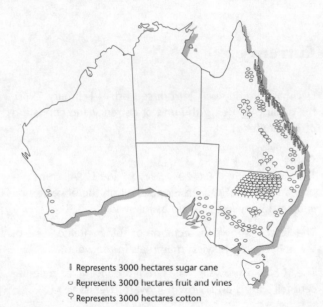

⌷ Represents 3000 hectares sugar cane

○ Represents 3000 hectares fruit and vines

♀ Represents 3000 hectares cotton

Currency

Decimal currency was introduced on 14 February 1966, the dollar (A$) being the unit of currency and consisting of 100 cents (¢).

Coins

The coins are: 5¢, 10¢, 20¢, 50¢, $1 and $2. All coins display an image of Queen Elizabeth II on the obverse side and on the reverse side are as follows:

The **5¢** coin shows the echidna or spiny anteater, one of the only two egg-laying mammals in the world.

The **10¢** coin shows a male lyrebird dancing, its magnificent tail spread and thrown forward over its head.

The **20¢** coin shows the platypus – the only other egg-laying mammal in the world.

The **50¢** coin shows the Commonwealth of Australia's coat of arms. This coin is sometimes minted with special designs for commemorative purposes.

The **$1** coin shows the kangaroo. It also has interrupted milling on the edge to assist visually impaired people.

The **$2** coin shows an Aborigine against a background of the Southern Cross.

Notes

There are five notes ($5, $10, $20, $50, $100), each a different colour and increasing in size with value. All depict personalities and themes of Australian historical interest.

They are all polymer (plastic) which allows the incorporation of sophisticated security features. The plastic notes were first introduced in 1992.

There are two **$5** notes. One features a portrait of Queen Elizabeth II on the front and Parliament House, Canberra on the back. The newer note, issued in 2001 to commemorate the Centenary of Federation, features Sir Henry Parkes, the 'Father of Federation', on the front and Catherine Spence, the first woman to stand for public office in Australia, on the back.

The **$10** note features a portrait of A. B. (Banjo) Paterson, surrounded by microprinted excerpts from his famous poem 'The Man from Snowy River' on the front. On the back is a portrait of poet and champion of the oppressed, Dame Mary Gilmore, surrounded by microprinted excerpts from her poem 'No Foe Shall Gather Our Harvest', with a bullock team in the background. The clear window has a windmill printed on it, along with embossed wave patterns.

The **$20** note features a portrait of Mary Reibey, who came to the colony as a convict, and later became a respected businesswoman. The reverse side commemorates the work of Reverend John Flynn, founder of the world-acclaimed Royal Flying Doctor Service. The clear window has a stylised compass printed in it, along with embossing of the number '20'.

The **$50** note features a portrait of David Unaipon, an inventor and Australia's first published Aboriginal author, on the front, and Edith Cowan, a social worker and Australia's first female parliamentarian, on the back. The clear window has a stylised version of the Southern Cross printed on it, along with embossing of the number '50'.

The **$100** note features a portrait of Dame Nellie Melba, one of Australia's best-known opera singers, and Sir John Monash, a soldier, engineer and administrator who is acknowledged for his outstanding leadership qualities in both military and civilian life. The clear window has a stylised image of a lyrebird and an embossed '100'.

State by State

Australian Capital Territory

Two areas transferred to the Commonwealth of Australia by the state of New South Wales originally made up the Australian Capital Territory (ACT). In 1908 the larger area around Canberra was chosen for the federal capital site, and in 1915 the smaller area of Jervis Bay on the New South Wales coast was transferred to the Commonwealth of Australia for development as a port. In 1993, after the formation of the ACT Legislative Assembly, the area around

Canberra was deemed the ACT and Jervis Bay remained Commonwealth territory.

Location
The ACT is in south-eastern New South Wales, west of the Great Dividing Range.

Area
The area of the ACT is 2538 square km.

Landform
Rolling plains and grasslands.

Population
315 589, mostly residents of Canberra.

Climate
Mainly temperate: cold nights and cool to very cold days in winter, warm to hot days and cool nights in summer. Average daily hours of sunshine: 7.2.

Administrative centre
Canberra is situated at the northern end of the ACT. It has an area of 805 square km and a population of 315 272, of which 28% are public servants.

Industry

In the ACT, government administration, health and cultural services account for 97.6% of production, and agriculture 2.4%.

Main attractions

Parliament House, Lake Burley Griffin, National Gallery of Australia, High Court of Australia, Captain Cook Memorial Water Jet, Red Hill, Black Mountain, Telstra Tower, Australian War Memorial, American War Memorial, foreign legations, Yarralumla (governor-general's residence), Vietnam War Memorial.

Major festivals

February	Royal Canberra Show
March	Canberra Festival
September	Floriade
October	Oktoberfest
	Canberra International Film Festival

DID YOU KNOW?
Walter Burley Griffin, an American landscape architect, came to Australia in 1913 after winning a worldwide design competition for Australia's new capital city, Canberra. He designed the city to follow the contours of the land and the buildings to blend into the natural setting.

New South Wales

Location

NSW lies in the south-east of the continent on the Pacific Ocean, with Queensland to the north and Victoria to the south.

Area

It is the fourth-largest state and is 801 600 square km (seven times larger than England).

Landform

Coastal slopes, plateaus and river flats are bounded by the Great Dividing Range, which runs north and south. West of the Dividing Range are rolling plains which deteriorate into semiarid desert.

Population

6 621 075 with the majority living in the three main cities: Sydney, Newcastle and Wollongong. Over half the state's population lives in Sydney.

Climate

Temperate and slightly humid in coastal areas with the deserts of the interior experiencing cold nights and hot days. Irregular floods and droughts occur. Average daily hours of sunshine: 6.7.

State capital

Sydney is built on Port Jackson, a sea inlet on the Pacific Ocean. The city has an area of 12 407 square km (including Penrith and Gosford), and a population of 4 163 531.

Largest cities

Sydney	4 163 531
Newcastle–Hunter	585 472
Wollongong–Illawarra	396 357
Wagga Wagga	56 753
Albury	48 910
Tamworth	37 109
Broken Hill	20 052

Industry

In New South Wales, health, education, cultural and other services, government and utilities account for 73% of the contribution to gross state product, the balance coming from manufacturing 13%, wholesale and retail 12%, with the remainder spread over mining and primary industry.

Chief products

Agriculture: wool, wheat, beef, cotton, mutton, dairy products, fruit, honey, poultry, sugar, timber.
Fishing: many varieties of fish and shellfish.
Manufacturing: agricultural implements, chemicals, clothing, fertiliser, glassware, iron and steel, machinery, motor cars, paper, textiles.
Mining: coal, copper, gold, lead, mineral sands, silver, zinc.

Main attractions

Sydney Harbour Bridge, Opera House, Darling Harbour, Rocks area, Olympic site at Homebush, Blue Mountains, Murrumbidgee Irrigation Area, Snowy Mountains, national parks, surfing beaches, fishing, wineries.

Flag

The New South Wales flag is based on the Blue Ensign with the state badge superimposed on the right-hand side. The badge consists of a golden lion on a red St George Cross within a white circle.

Coat of Arms

The present coat of arms was approved in 1906 by King Edward VII. It consists of a shield with the red cross of St George supported by a lion and a kangaroo. The motto is 'Newly risen, how brightly you shine'.

Emblems

Animal: platypus
Floral: waratah
Bird: kookaburra

Major festivals

January	Festival of Sydney
	Tamworth Country Music Festival
February	Sydney Gay & Lesbian Mardi Gras
October	Bathurst 1000 car race
	Newcastle Mattara Festival

DID YOU KNOW?
Sydney Tower, at Centrepoint, is the highest building in the southern hemisphere, 324.8 metres above sea level.

Victoria

Location
Victoria lies in the south-eastern corner of the continent

Area
It is the smallest state on the mainland and is 227 600 square km in area.

Landform
Mountainous areas in the north-east, and semiarid areas in the north-west. Most land is well suited to farming, and as a result Victoria is often referred to as the 'garden state'.

Population
4 851 154. Victoria is the most densely populated and most highly urbanised of all the states.

Climate

Generally temperate although the climate is subject to wide variation. High rainfall, extremes of summer heat and irregular floods and droughts occur. Average daily hours of sunshine: 5.7.

State capital

Melbourne is situated on the Yarra River, on Port Phillip Bay. It has an area of 6109 square km and a population of 3 520 503 (about 70% of the state's population). Melbourne's motto is *Vires acquirit eundo* or 'We gather strength as we grow'.

Largest cities

Melbourne	3 520 503
Geelong and environs	191 538
Ballarat	82 693
Bendigo	78 265
Shepparton	42 879

Industry

In Victoria, health, education, cultural and other services, government and utilities account for 65% of the contribution to gross state product, the balance coming from manufacturing 16%, wholesale and retail 11%, with the remainder spread over mining and primary industry.

Chief products

Agriculture: cattle, forest products, fruit, hay and straw, milk and dairy products, poultry and eggs, sheep, vegetables, wheat, wool.
Manufacturing: building materials, chemical products, clothing, farm machinery, footwear, light engineering, motor vehicles, textiles.
Mining: brown coal, natural gas, oil.

Main attractions

Melbourne Cup, Australian Rules Football, National Tennis Centre, Formula One Grand Prix, Phillip Island (penguins), wineries, prospecting, riverboat cruising, surfing, snowfields, national parks, sailing, fishing.

Flag

Victoria was the first state to have its own flag. The flag is made up of the Blue Ensign with the badge of the state which consists of five white stars of the Southern Cross in the fly with a crown above.

Coat of arms

The present coat of arms was granted by Queen Elizabeth II in 1972. It incorporates a shield of five stars representing the constellation of the Southern Cross. On either side stands a female figure, one representing peace and the other prosperity. The motto is 'Peace and prosperity'.

Emblems
Animal: Leadbeater's possum
Floral: pink heath

Major festivals

January	Australian Open Tennis
March	Melbourne Moomba Festival
	Melbourne Formula One Grand Prix
Easter	Stawell Gift foot race
April/May	Bright Autumn Festival
	500cc Motorcycle Grand Prix at Phillip Island
September	Australian Football League Grand Final
Sept/Oct	Tesselaar's Tulip Festival, Silvan
October	Melbourne Festival
November	Melbourne Cup

DID YOU KNOW?
The Yarra River, an important waterway and part of Melbourne's water supply, flows 250 km from Mt Baw Baw in the Great Dividing Range, south-west to its estuary in Port Phillip Bay. Baw Baw is an Aboriginal word meaning 'running water'.

Queensland

Location

Queensland lies on the north-east of the continent, bordering the Pacific Ocean to the east, and Torres Strait to the north.

Area

Second-largest state: 1 727 200 square km.

Landform

The north coast is sheltered by islands and the Great Barrier Reef system. Behind the coastal slopes of the Great Dividing Range and river flats, are rolling plains, then the land becomes semiarid desert.

Population

3 724 840, mostly in four coastal areas.

Climate

The climate is mostly tropical with two main seasons – wet and dry. Queensland is known as the 'sunshine state' because of pleasantly warm winters and long hours of sunshine. Average daily hours of sunshine: 7.5.

State capital

Brisbane is situated on the Brisbane River on the east coast. It has an area of 3080 square km and a population of 1 659 586.

Largest cities

Brisbane	1 659 586
Gold Coast and environs	371 785
Cairns and environs	120 573
Ipswich	120 453
Townsville	91 613
Toowoomba	87 934

Industry

In Queensland, health, education, cultural and other services, government and utilities account for 65% of the contribution to gross state product, the balance coming from manufacturing 11%, wholesale and retail 13%, with the remainder spread over mining and primary industry.

Chief products

Agriculture: barley, cattle, cotton, fruit, maize, peanuts, pigs, sheep, sugar, tobacco, wheat, wool.
Fishing: many varieties of fish, prawns.
Manufacturing: aerated waters, basic metal products, brick-making, dairy products, electricity generation, meat products, ready-mixed concrete, timber processing.
Mining: bauxite, coal, copper, gold, lead, mineral sands, nickel, salt, tin, uranium, zinc.

Main attractions

The Great Barrier Reef (a complex organic system and one of the greatest biological wonders of the world), Gold Coast, Sunshine Coast, Cape York Peninsula, Indy car race, surf beaches, fishing, tropical islands, prospecting, national parks, rainforests, whale-watching.

Flag

The flag is based on the Blue Ensign with the state badge superimposed on the right-hand side. It has a blue Maltese Cross with the Imperial Crown in the centre. This badge was proclaimed in 1876.

Coat of arms

The present coat of arms was granted by Queen Elizabeth

II in 1977. It consists of a shield with pictures representing pastoral, mining and agricultural industries. This is supported by a red deer and the brolga. The motto means 'Bold, aye, but faithful too'.

Emblems

Animal: koala
Floral: Cooktown orchid

Major festivals

August	Royal Brisbane Show ('The Ekka')
September	Mackay's Sugartime Festival
	Toowoomba Carnival of Flowers
October	Cairns Fun in the Sun Festival
	Ipswich Country Music Festival
	Rockhampton Arts in the Park
December	Woodford Folk Festival

DID YOU KNOW?
The world's largest structure created by living creatures is the Great Barrier Reef. It extends along the Queensland coast for more than 2000 km and covers an area of almost 260 000 square km.

South Australia

Location

South Australia occupies a central position on the southern coastline. Seaward is the Great Australian Bight.

Area

It is the third-largest state and covers one-eighth of the total area of Australia. It is 984 000 square km in area, with a coastline of 3700 km.

Landform

Undulating hills, grasslands and valleys; semiarid to arid deserts in the north.

Population

Sparsely populated with 1 510 062 people mainly concentrated in the south-east corner of the state.

Climate

Mostly a Mediterranean climate, warm to hot in summer and cool in winter. It is the driest state with four-fifths of its total area receiving less than 254 mm of rainfall a year. Average daily hours of sunshine: 6.9.

State capital

Adelaide, situated on the Torrens River in St Vincent Gulf, is sheltered by the Mt Lofty Range. The population is 1 103 812 and its area is 1870 square km.

Largest cities and towns

Adelaide	1 103 812
Elizabeth	25 641
Mt Gambier	23 592
Whyalla	23 280
Port Pirie	17 619
Port Augusta	13 441

Industry

In South Australia, health, education, cultural and other services, government and utilities account for 66% of the contribution to gross state product, the balance coming from manufacturing 16%, wholesale and retail 11%, with the remainder spread over mining and primary industry.

Chief products

Agriculture: almonds, barley, beef, dairy products, fruits, vegetables, wheat, wine, wool.
Manufacturing: carriages and wagons, chemicals, cotton, electrical goods, iron and steel, machinery, motor cars, pipes.
Mining: barytes, coal, copper, dolomite, gypsum, iron ore, natural gas, opals, salt, talc.

Main attractions

Vineyards in Barossa Valley and Clare Valley, Flinders Ranges, opal fields, Blue Lake/Mt Gambier, Kangaroo Island, Moonta and Burra Burra copper mine sites, The Barrages at Goolwa, Victor Harbor, Nullarbor Plain, Great Australian Bight Marine Park, whale-watching.

Flag

Based on the Blue Ensign with the state badge superimposed on the right-hand side. It consists of a piping shrike with wings outstretched on a yellow background.

Coat of arms

The present coat of arms was conferred by Queen Elizabeth II in 1984. It incorporates objects representing all aspects of industry in South Australia. At the base is a scroll with the words 'South Australia'.

Emblems
Animal: hairy-nosed wombat
Floral: Sturt's desert pea

Major festivals

January	Adelaide Schützenfest
	Tanunda Oompah Festival
February	Adelaide Festival of the Arts
	(even-numbered years)
April	Barossa Valley Vintage Festival
	(odd-numbered years)
May	Kernewek Lowender
	(odd numbered years)
	Adelaide Cup Racing Festival
November	Adelaide Christmas Pageant
December	Proclamation Day

DID YOU KNOW?
In 1862 John McDouall Stuart won 2000 pounds for
finding a possible route between South Australia
and the northern coastline. The Postmaster General
of South Australia offered the reward in an
attempt to establish an overland telegraph. This
was completed in 1872.

Western Australia

Western Australia occupies the western third of the continent bordered by the Indian Ocean in the west and the Southern Ocean in the south.

Area

It is the largest state in Australia and is 2 252 500 square km in area.

Landform

The state extends from vast arable southern areas to semi-arid and arid landscapes in the interior and the mineral-rich Great Sandy and Gibson deserts to the north. The mountain ranges are Stirling, Kimberley and Hamersley.

Population

1 962 030 (concentrated on the south-west coast), representing only 9% of the total Australian population. The

large desert and semiarid areas are unsuitable for cultivation or close settlement.

Climate

Western Australia has three broad climate divisions. The northern part is dry tropical, receiving summer rainfall. The south-western corner has a Mediterranean climate with long hot summers and wet winters. The remainder is mostly arid land with desert climates. Average daily hours of sunshine: 7.9.

State capital

Perth is situated on the Swan River on the seaboard of the Indian Ocean. It is 5306 square km in area and has a population of 1 395 416.

Largest cities

Perth	1 395 416
Boulder–Kalgoorlie	31 939
Fremantle	42 218
Bunbury	29 741
Geraldton	19 861
Albany	15 980
Port Hedland	13 272

Industry

In Western Australia, health, education, cultural and other services, government and utilities account for 58% of the contribution to gross state product, the balance coming from mining 20%, wholesale and retail 9%, manufacturing 9% and primary industry 4%.

Chief products

Agriculture: cattle, fruit, hardwoods, rock lobsters, wheat, wool.
Manufacturing: building materials, food and drink, metal, machinery, other mineral products, petroleum products, wood products.
Mining: bauxite, gold, ilmenite, iron ore, nickel, oil, salt.

Main attractions

Margaret River wine and cave region, Kalgoorlie gold-fields, Esperance, Rottnest Island, Kimberley and Hamersley ranges, Broome, surfing, fishing, sailing, wildflowers, Monkey Mia (dolphins), Pinnacle Desert, Bungle Bungles, Wave Rock near Hyden.

Flag

The flag is based on the Blue Ensign with the badge of the

state superimposed on the right-hand side. It has a black swan within a yellow circle.

Coat of arms

The present coat of arms was granted by Queen Elizabeth II in 1969. It incorporates a shield depicting a black swan, the bird emblem of the state. It is supported by two kangaroos each holding a boomerang.

Emblems

Animal: numbat
Floral: red and green kangaroo paw

Major festivals

January	Mandurah Festival
February	Festival of Perth
April	Albany Festival
August	Tom Price Nameless Festival
November	Fremantle Festival
	Margaret River Wine Region Festival

DID YOU KNOW?
In 1975, at Onslow in Western Australia, the wind velocity reached 246 km/h – the strongest wind ever recorded in Australia.

Tasmania

Location

The island state lies 240 km off the south-eastern corner of the Australian continent and is separated from the mainland by Bass Strait.

Area

Tasmania is the smallest state in Australia, with an area of 68 331 square km. The island measures 286 km north to south.

Landform

Mountainous with many lakes, waterfalls and steeply falling rivers, and vast tracts of wilderness.

Population

467 294, mostly in the south and north-west.

Climate

Cool temperate with temperatures often falling below zero. High rainfall, very cold winters and cool summers. Average daily hours of sunshine: 5.8.

State capital

Hobart, the second-oldest city in Australia, is situated on the Derwent River on the Tasman Peninsula. It has an area of 936 square km and a population of 192 615.

Largest cities

Hobart	192 615
Launceston	97 767
Burnie and Devonport	73 367

Industry

In Tasmania, health, education, cultural and other services, government and utilities account for 67% of the contribution to gross state product, the balance coming from manufacturing 16%, wholesale and retail 10%, with the remainder spread over mining and primary industry.

Chief products

Agriculture: beef, fruit, dairy products, hops, lavender, mutton, potatoes, timber, wool.
Fishing: barracouta, crayfish, salmon, scallops.
Manufacturing: alginate, aluminium, frozen food, canned fruit, paper, pulp.
Mining: coal, copper, gold, iron, lead, tin, zinc.

Main attractions

Snowfields, unspoiled mountain landscapes, historical places, national parks, Franklin River, seascapes, thermal pools, Cradle Mountain, Gordon River, fishing, bushwalking.

Flag

Based on the Blue Ensign with the badge of the state superimposed on the right-hand side. It consists of a red lion in a white circle.

Coat of arms

The present coat of arms was granted by King George V in 1917. On the shield are pictures representing industry in Tasmania. This is supported by two Tasmanian tigers. The motto means 'Productiveness and faithfulness'.

Emblem

Floral: southern blue gum

Major festivals

January	Arrival of Sydney-to-Hobart Yacht Race
	Great Tasmanian Bike Ride
March	Devonport Regatta
April	Statewide National Heritage Week
October	Burnie Rhododendron Festival
	Royal Hobart Agricultural Show
	Launceston Garden Festival
December	Hobart Salamanca Arts Festival

DID YOU KNOW?
**Because Tasmanian bees are exclusive to the island
and the pollen of the flowers is kept relatively pure,
Tasmanian honey has a unique and distinctive taste.**

Northern Territory

Location

The Northern Territory occupies a huge area of the continent's north and centre. It is bordered by the Timor Sea to the north, Queensland to the east, Western Australia to the west and South Australia to the south. Usually known as 'Outback Australia'.

Area

Comprises one-sixth of Australia's land mass and is 1 346 200 square km in area.

Landform

Mostly desert and tablelands.

Population

205 773. Few people live in the huge dry areas and almost half the population are residents of Darwin. More than one quarter of the people are Aborigines.

Climate

The Northern Territory lies in the torrid zone. There are two broad climatic divisions: the northern part known as the 'Top End' receives heavy rainfall for three to five months of the year and the southern area, known as 'The Centre', has a low rainfall and no permanent rivers. Average daily hours of sunshine: 8.5.

Administrative centre

Darwin is situated in Beagle Gulf on the Timor Sea and is 1660 square km in area. It has a population of 91 324.

Chief towns

Darwin	91 324
Alice Springs	38 375
Katherine	10 172
Tennant Creek	5 983
Nhulunbuy	3 458

Industry

In the Northern Territory, health, education, cultural and other services, government and utilities account for 67% of the contribution to gross state product, the balance coming from mining 18%, wholesale and retail 8%, manufacturing 4% and primary industry 3%.

Chief products

Agriculture: beef cattle, citrus fruits, lucerne, peanuts, pineapples, timber, tomatoes.
Fishing: fish and prawns.
Mining: aluminium, bauxite, copper, gold, iron, manganese, tin, uranium.

Main attractions

Kata Tjuta National Park (Mt Olga), Kings Canyon, Standley Chasm, The Ghan (train from Adelaide to Alice Springs), Katherine Gorge, Bathurst and Melville islands, Kakadu National Park, Uluru National Park (Ayers Rock), Devil's Marbles, Mataranka thermal pools, Litchfield National Park.

Flag

The flag of the Northern Territory is not based on the Blue Ensign. Instead, traditional Territory colours are used: black, white and red ochre. The stars on the black panel represent the Southern Cross. On the red ochre panel appears Sturt's desert rose.

Coat of arms

The present coat of arms was granted by Queen Elizabeth II in 1978. It incorporates a shield depicting an Arnhem Land rock painting of an Aboriginal woman. The shield is supported by two red kangaroos. The crest consists of a wedge-tailed eagle with wings splayed and its talons grasping an Aboriginal ritual stone or *tjurunga*.

Emblems

Animal: red kangaroo
Floral: Sturt's desert rose

Major festivals

May	Alice Springs Bangtail Muster
	Tennant Creek Cup Day
June	Barunga Cultural and Sports Festival (Katherine)
August	Darwin Beer Can Regatta
September	Festival of Darwin
October	Alice Springs Henley-on-Todd Regatta

DID YOU KNOW?
Alice Springs is almost the geographical centre of the continent in the great central desert. It is the focal point for the arid inland, more popularly known as the 'red centre'.

Famous Australians

There have been thousands of famous Australians. Here is a very modest list of talented Australians, past and present, who have helped make this country what it is today.

Architects
Francis Greenway *(1777–1837)*
Colonel William Light *(1786–1839)*
Edmund Blacket *(1817–83)*
Sir Roy Grounds *(1905–81)*
Robin Boyd *(1919–71)*
Harry Seidler *(1923–)*
Glenn Murcutt *(1936–)*

Aviators
Lawrence Hargrave *(1850–1915)*
Keith Smith *(1890–1955)*
Sir Hudson Fysh *(1895–1974)*

Ross Smith *(1892–1922)*
Bert Hinkler *(1892–1933)*
Sir Charles Kingsford Smith *(1897–1935)*
Amy Johnson *(1903–41)*
Sir Reginald Ansett *(1909–81)*
Andy Thomas *(1951–)*

Businesspeople
John Macarthur *(1767–1834)*
Sir Sidney Kidman *(1897–1935)*
Sir Warwick Fairfax *(1901–87)*
Herbert Cole 'Nugget' Coombs *(1906–97)*
Lang Hancock *(1909–92)*
Rupert Murdoch *(1931–)*
Robert Holmes à Court *(1937–90)*
Kerry Packer *(1937–)*
Dick Smith *(1944–)*

Cartoonists
Stan Cross *(1888–1977)*
Emile Mercier *(c. 1909–81)*
Frank Benier *(c. 1923–)*
Bruce Petty *(1929–)*
Ron Tandberg *(1943–)*
Michael Leunig *(1945–)*

Engineers & inventors

William James Farrer *(1845–1906)*
Herbert Lysaght *(1862–1940)*
John Bradfield *(1867–1943)*
Walter Hume *(1873–1943)*
Essington Lewis *(1881–1961)*
Mervyn Victor Richardson *(1894–1972)*
John Paul Wild *(1923–)*
Ralph Sarich *(1938–)*

Scientists & medicos

William Redfern *(c. 1774–1833)*
Reverend John Flynn *(1880–1951)*
Baron (Howard) Florey *(1898–1968)*
Sir Marcus Oliphant *(1901–2000)*
Sir John Eccles *(1903–1997)*
Sir Edward 'Weary' Dunlop *(1907–93)*
Professor Fred Hollows *(1929–93)*
Dr Victor Chang *(c. 1940–91)*
Dr Peter Doherty *(1940–)*
Professor Suzanne Cory *(1942–)*
Dr Eric LePage *(1958–)*

Literature

Novelists and writers

Henry Handel Richardson *(1870–1946)*
Miles Franklin *(1879–1954)*

Xavier Herbert *(1901–84)*
Patrick White *(1912–90)*
Frank Hardy *(1917–94)*
Elizabeth Jolley *(1923–)*
Thea Astley *(1925–)*
Ruth Park *(1926–)*
David Ireland *(1927–)*
Christopher Koch *(1932–)*
Bryce Courtenay *(1933–)*
David Malouf *(1934–)*
Thomas Keneally *(1935–)*
Helen Garner *(1942–)*
Peter Carey *(1943–)*
Kate Grenville *(1950–)*
Tim Winton *(1960–)*

Playwrights

Ray Lawler *(1922–)*
Richard Beynon *(1925–1999)*
Peter Kenna *(1930–)*
David Williamson *(1942–)*
Alexander Buzo *(1944–)*
Louis Nowra *(1950–)*

Poets

Andrew Barton 'Banjo' Paterson *(1864–1941)*
Dame Mary Gilmore *(1865–1962)*

Henry Lawson *(1867–1922)*
C. J. Dennis *(1876–1938)*
Kenneth Slessor *(1901–71)*
A. D. Hope *(1907–2000)*
Douglas Stewart *(1913–85)*
Judith Wright *(1915–2000)*
Oodgeroo of the tribe Noonuccal (formerly Kath Walker) *(1920–93)*
Les Murray *(1938–)*

Theatre
J. C. Williamson *(1835–1913)*
Leo McKern *(1921–2002)*
Ruth Cracknell *(1925–2002)*
June Salter *(1932–)*
John Meillon *(1934–90)*
Barry Humphries *(1934–)*
John Bell *(1940–)*
Max Cullen *(1941–)*
Robyn Nevin *(1942–)*
John Waters *(1945–)*
Jacki Weaver *(1947–)*
Garry McDonald *(1948–)*

Radio
John Laws *(1935–)*
Bob Francis *(1938–)*
Margaret Throsby *(1942–)*

Bill Gates *(c. 1945–)*
Jeremy Cordeaux *(1945–)*
Howard Sattler *(1945–)*
Alan Jones *(c. 1947–)*
Ian 'Macca' MacNamara *(1947–)*
Neil Mitchell *(1951–)*

Television

Hector Crawford *(1914–91)*
Brian Henderson *(1931–)*
Ernie Sigley *(1938–)*
Bert Newton *(1938–)*
Lorraine Bayly *(1939–)*
Mike Willesee *(1942–)*
John Clarke *(c. 1943–)*
Ray Martin *(1944–)*
Don Burke *(1948–)*
Daryl Somers *(1952–)*
Ernie Dingo *(1957–)*
Peter Phelps *(c. 1965–)*
Lisa McCune *(1971–)*

Film

Silent movies
Bert Bailey *(1872–1953)*
Arthur Tauchert *(1877–1933)*
Lottie Lyell *(1891–1925)*
George Wallace *(1894–1960)*

Early Talkies

Errol Flynn *(1909–59)*
Chips Rafferty *(1909–71)*
Peter Finch *(1915–77)*

Contemporary

Bill Hunter *(1939–)*
Paul Hogan *(1939–)*
Bryan Brown *(1947–)*
Sam Neill *(1947–)*
Geoffrey Rush *(1950–)*
Colin Friels *(1953–)*
Judy Davis *(1956–)*
Mel Gibson *(1956–)*
Greta Scacchi *(1960–)*
Hugo Weaving *(1960–)*
Russell Crowe *(1964–)*
Nicole Kidman *(1967–)*
Hugh Jackman *(1968–)*
Frances O'Connor *(1969–)*
Noah Taylor *(1969–)*
Cate Blanchett *(1969–)*
Rachel Griffiths *(1968–)*
Ben Mendelsohn *(1969–)*
Miranda Otto *(1967–)*
Toni Collette *(1972–)*

Matt Day *(1971–)*
Guy Pearce *(1967–)*

Film-makers

Patricia Lovell *(c. 1932–)*
Fred Schepisi *(1939–)*
Bruce Beresford *(1940–)*
Dean Semler *(1943–)*
Peter Weir *(1944–)*
George Miller *(1949–)*
Phillip Noyce *(1950–)*
Gillian Armstrong *(1950–)*
Rolf de Heer *(1951–)*
Laura Jones *(1951–)*
Jane Campion *(1954–)*
Baz Luhrmann *(1962–)*

Contemporary music
Rock

Johnny O'Keefe *(1935–78)*
Billy Thorpe *(c. 1940–)*
Jimmy Barnes *(1946–)*
Daryl Braithwaite *(1949–)*
John Farnham *(1949–)*
Ian Moss *(1950–)*
Paul Kelly *(1955–)*

Archie Roach *(1956–)*
Jenny Morris *(1957–)*
Nick Cave *(1957–)*
Wendy Matthews *(1960–)*
Kate Ceberano *(1966–)*
Tina Arena *(1967–)*
Kylie Minogue *(1968–)*
Christine Anu *(c. 1973–)*
Natalie Imbruglia *(1975–)*

Country

Smoky Dawson *(1913–)*
Slim Dusty *(1927–)*
Reg Lindsay *(1929–)*
Jimmy Little *(1935–)*
Anne Kirkpatrick *(1952–)*
Graeme Connors *(1955–)*
Colin Buchanan *(1964–)*
Lee Kernaghan *(1964–)*
James Blundell *(1965–)*
Jane Saunders *(1965–)*
Darren Coggan *(c. 1967–)*
Troy Cassar-Daley *(1968–)*
Gina Jeffreys *(1968–)*
Adam Brand *(c. 1975–)*
Kasey Chambers *(1976–)*

Rock bands

AC/DC
Air Supply
Angels
Australian Crawl
Baby Animals
Bee Gees
Black Sorrows
Bodyjar
Chocolate Starfish
Cold Chisel
Crowded House
Daddy Cool
Divinyls
Easybeats
Even
Hoodoo Gurus
Hunters and Collectors
Icehouse
INXS
Killing Heidi
Little River Band

Men at Work
Mental as Anything
Midnight Oil
Newsboys
Noiseworks
Powderfinger
Regurgitator
Savage Garden
Screaming Jets
Sherbet
silverchair
Skyhooks
Southern Sons
The Superjesus
Tiddas
Weddings, Parties,
   Anything
Whitlams
Yothu Yindi
You Am I

Other performers

Tommy Tycho *(1929–)*
Peter Allen *(1944–92)*
Eric Bogle *(1944–)*
John Williamson *(1945–)*
Julie Anthony *(1951–)*
Tommy Emmanuel *(1955–)*
Debbie Byrne *(1958–)*
Dein Perry *(1959–)*
James Morrison *(1963–)*
Anthony Warlow *(1964–)*
Marina Prior *(1964–)*

Classical music
Percy Grainger *(1882–1961)*
Peter Sculthorpe *(1929–)*
Richard Bonynge *(1930–)*
Nigel Butterley *(1935–)*
John Williams *(1941–)*
Roger Woodward *(1942–)*
Simone Young *(1961–)*
Karin Schaupp *(c. 1975–)*

Ballet & dance
Sir Robert Helpmann *(1909–86)*
Marilyn Jones *(1940–)*

Marilyn Rowe-Maver *(1946–)*
Graeme Murphy *(1950–)*
Garry Norman *(1951–)*
David Atkins *(1956–)*
Meryl Tankard *(c. 1957–)*
Lisa Pavane *(1962–)*
Greg Horsman *(1963–)*
Adam Marchant *(1963–)*
Steven Heathcote *(1965–)*
David McAllister *(1965–)*
Miranda Coney *(1966–)*
Paul Mercurio *(c. 1967–)*
Vicki Attard *(c. 1967–)*
Damien Welch *(c. 1972–)*
Justine Summers *(c. 1974–)*
Lisa Bolte *(c. 1975–)*

Opera
Dame Nellie Melba *(1861–1931)*
Donald Smith *(1920–88)*
Dame Joan Sutherland *(1926–)*
Heather Begg *(1933–)*
Joan Carden *(c. 1937–)*
Donald Shanks *(1940–)*
Yvonne Kenny *(c. 1951–)*
Graham Pushee *(c. 1955–)*

Peter Coleman-Wright *(1959–)*
Cheryl Barker *(1960–)*

Art

Frederick McCubbin *(1855–1917)*
Tom Roberts *(1856–1931)*
Max Meldrum *(1875–1955)*
Margaret Preston *(1875–1963)*
Norman Lindsay *(1879–1969)*
Sali Herman *(1898–1993)*
Albert Namatjira *(1902–59)*
Sir Sidney Nolan *(1917–92)*
Arthur Boyd *(1920–99)*
Judy Cassab *(1920–)*
Robert Klippel *(1920–)*
Margaret Olley *(1922–)*
Sam Fullbrook *(1922–)*
Fred Williams *(1927–82)*
Colin Lanceley *(1938–)*
Brett Whiteley *(1939–92)*
Trevor Nicholls *(1949–)*
Tim Storrier *(1949–)*
Judy Watson *(1959–)*

Major Australian films 1970–2002

1971	*Wake in Fright*
1972	*The Adventures of Barry McKenzie*
1973	*Alvin Purple*
1974	*The Cars That Ate Paris*
1975	*Picnic at Hanging Rock*
	The Removalists
1976	*Caddie*
	Don's Party
1977	*The Getting of Wisdom*
1978	*My Brilliant Career*
	Newsfront
	The Chant of Jimmie Blacksmith
1979	*Mad Max*
	Breaker Morant
1981	*Puberty Blues*
1982	*Gallipoli*
	The Man from Snowy River
	The Year of Living Dangerously
1983	*Careful, He Might Hear You*
1984	*My First Wife*
1985	*Bliss*
	Empty Beach
1986	*Backlash*
	Crocodile Dundee
	The Fringe Dwellers

1987	*Boundaries of the Heart*
	The Year My Voice Broke
1988	*Crocodile Dundee II*
	Dead Calm
1989	*Jig Saw*
	Sweetie
1990	*The Crossing*
	Flirting
1991	*Death in Brunswick*
1992	*Strictly Ballroom*
	Romper Stomper
1993	*The Piano*
1994	*The Adventures of Priscilla, Queen of the Desert*
	Muriel's Wedding
1995	*Lillian's Story*
	Babe
	Così
1996	*Shine*
	Love Serenade
	Love and Other Catastrophes
1997	*The Castle*
	True Love and Chaos
	The Quiet Room
	Doing Time for Patsy Cline
	Kiss or Kill
	Oscar and Lucinda

1998	*In the Winter Dark*
	The Sound of One Hand Clapping
	The Boys
	Dance Me to My Song
1999	*Paperback Hero*
	The Craic
	In a Savage Land
	Siam Sunset
	Two Hands
2000	*Chopper*
	Looking for Alibrandi
	The Dish
	Mallboy
2001	*Lantana*
	Moulin Rouge
	The Man Who Sued God
	Yolngu Boy
2002	*Rabbit-Proof Fence*
	Beneath Clouds
	Dirty Deeds
	The Hard Word

Sporting Greats

Australia is a very enthusiastic sporting nation. We love our sport, whether watching or playing. Over the years we have had countless sporting legends who have shone in many different sports. Obviously, a book this size cannot hope to do justice to them all, so here are just some of them.

Tennis

Lawn tennis was first introduced in the 1870s and the first Australian championship was in 1905. The first Davis Cup challenge was in 1906. Tennis has become one of Australia's most popular sports. The following list names some of the greats:

1900–40s

Norman Brookes
Jack Crawford
Harry Hopman
Gerald Patterson
Adrian Quist

1950s–70s

John Bromwich
Evonne Cawley (Goolagong)
Roy Emerson
Neale Fraser
Lew Hoad
Rod Laver
Ken McGregor
John Newcombe
Tony Roche
Ken Rosewall
Frank Sedgman
Margaret Smith Court

1980s–2000s

Wayne Arthurs
Pat Cash
Scott Draper

Annabel Ellwood
Kerri-Ann Guse
Lleyton Hewitt
Peter McNamara
Paul McNamee
Rachel McQuillan
Mark Philippoussis
Nicole Pratt
Patrick Rafter
Sandon Stolle
Jason Stoltenberg
Wendy Turnbull
Todd Woodbridge
Mark Woodforde

Cricket

The first organised match was held in Sydney in 1803. The Australian Club was formed in 1826 and the Melbourne Cricket Club in 1838. International cricket began in 1861.

1900–40s

G. W. Armstrong
Don Bradman
Bill Hunt
M. A. Noble

Bill O'Reilly
W. H. Ponsford
Hugh Trumble
Victor Trumper

1950s–60s
Richie Benaud
Ian Craig
Wally Grout
Neil Harvey
Lindsay Hassett
Bill Lawry
Ray Lindwall
Keith Miller
Bob Simpson

1970s–2000s
David Boon
Allan Border
Greg Chappell
Ian Chappell
Adam Gilchrist
Ian Healy
Merv Hughes
Dennis Lillee

Geoff Marsh
Rod Marsh
Craig McDermott
Glenn McGrath
Mark Taylor
Shane Warne
Mark Waugh
Steve Waugh

Golf

Australians have more public courses per head than any other nation. The game was first played in the 1870s and in 1890 the first established golf club was at Fallstaff Gardens in Melbourne.

1920s–1940s

Jim Ferrier
Joan Hammond
Joe Kirkwood
Norman von Nida
Ivo Whitton

1950s–1970s

Bruce Crampton
Bruce Devlin

Edwina Kennedy
Kel Nagle
Jack Newton
Peter Thomson

1980s–2000s

Robert Allenby
Stuart Appleby
Ian Baker-Finch
Roger Davis
Steve Elkington
Michelle Ellis
David Graham
Bradley Hughes
Graham Marsh
Greg Norman
Craig Parry
Adam Scott
Peter Senior
Bob Shearer
Craig Spence
Jan Stephenson
Rachel Teske
Karrie Webb

Swimming

Because of our wonderful climate and beautiful beaches, Australians have always loved swimming. Swimming racing gained international fame when the 'Australian Crawl' (now called freestyle) was introduced in the 1890s.

1900–30s

Frank Beaurepaire
Dick Cavill
Fred Cavill
Andrew ('Boy') Charlton
Claire Dennis
Fanny Durack
Annette Kellerman
Barney Bede Kieran
Freddy Lane
Bill Longworth

1940s–60s

Kevin Berry
Gary Chapman
Lorraine Crapp
John Devitt
Dawn Fraser

Jon Henricks
Ilsa Konrads
John Konrads
Lynette McClements
Linda McGill
John Marshall
Ian O'Brien
Murray Rose
David Thiele
Mike Wenden
Robert Windle

1970s–80s

Duncan Armstrong
Clifford Bertram
Neil Brooks
Brad Cooper
Lisa Curry
Michelle Ford
Shane Gould
Gail Neal
Des Renford
Jon Sieben
Beverley Whitfield
Tracey Wickham

1990s–2000s

Rebecca Brown
Grant Hackett
Leisel Jones
Michael Klim
Daniel Kowalski
Susie Maroney
David O'Brien
Susie O'Neill
Todd Pearson
Kieren Perkins
Samantha Riley
Giann Rooney
Shelley Taylor-Smith
Petria Thomas
Ian Thorpe
Joseph Walker
Tammy van Wisse

Australian Football League (AFL)

The game was devised in 1858 by cricketers as a form of exercise in their off-season. It has now become one of the most popular spectator sports in Australia. The AFL has inducted 17 legends into its Hall of Fame.

Roy Cazaly *(1910–27)*
Gordon Coventry *(1920–37)*
Bob Pratt *(1930–46)*
Jack Dyer *(1931–49)*
Haydn Bunton *(1931–41)*
Dick Reynolds *(1933–51)*
John Coleman *(1949–54)*
Ted Whitten *(1951–70)*
Ron Barassi *(1955–77)*
Bob Skilton *(1956–71)*
Graham 'Polly' Farmer *(1956–60)*
John Nicholls *(1957–74)*
Ian Stewart *(1963–75)*
Kevin Bartlett *(1965–83)*
Barrie Robran *(1967–80)*
Leigh Matthews *(1969–85)*
Peter Hudson *(1969–80)*

National Rugby League (NRL)

The first Kangaroo team toured England in 1908–09 and won their first test in 1911–12. The Kangaroos have won the World Cup eight times out of the eleven tournaments played. Some greats of the game and the years they played are:

Herbert (Dally) Messenger *(1908–13)*
Duncan Thompson *(1911–25)*
Frank Burge *(1911–27)*
Harold Horder *(1912–26)*
Dave Brown *(1930–41)*
Vic Hey *(1933–49)*
Clive Churchill *(1951–63)*
John Raper *(1957–73)*
Ken Irvine *(1958–72)*
Reg Gasnier *(1959–67)*
Graeme Langlands *(1962–76)*
Keith 'Golden Boots' Barnes *(1963–70)*
Ron Coote *(1965–78)*
Bob Fulton *(1965–79)*
Arthur Beetson *(1966–81)*
Tom Radonikus *(1976–85)*
Wally Lewis *(1978–92)*
Mal Meninga *(1978–94)*
Peter Sterling *(1978–92)*

Allan Langer *(1986–99)*
Laurie Daley *(1987–)*
Ricky Stuart *(1988–)*
Brad Fittler *(1989–)*
Andrew Johns *(1989–)*

Rugby Union

Rugby Union was first played in Australia in 1864. The first Wallabies team won gold at the 1908 London Olympics. The Wallabies won the World Cup Grand Slam tour in 1984 defeating England, Scotland, Wales and Ireland and in 1991 won the second World Cup championships. It remains an amateur game. Some great names from the last three decades are:

Andrew Slack
Mark Ella
David Campese
Michael Lynagh
Nick Farr-Jones
John Eales
Tim Horan
Phil Kearns
David Wilson

Soccer

The game was played as early as 1880 but only gained popularity when the Australian team, the Socceroos, qualified for the first time in the 1974 World Cup finals. The Socceroos have reached the finals of the Seoul, Barcelona and Atlanta Olympics. Some of Australia's soccer legends are:

Atti Abonyi
Mark Bosnich
Branko Buljevic
Alan Davidson
Craig Johnston
Harry Kewell
John Kosmina
Eddie Krncevic
Jim Mackay
Joe Marston
Peter Ollerton
Jack Reilly
Jimmy Rooney
Paul Wade
Johnny Warren
Harry Williams
Peter Wilson
Charlie Yankos
Ned Zelic

Boxing

Bare-knuckle fights were staged in the 1790s but the rules were standardised in 1912. Some of the past century's greats (and the dates they competed) are:

Bill Squires *(1906–8)*
Jerry Jerome *(1913)*
Les Darcy *(1914–16)*
Colin Bell *(1921)*
Billy Grime *(1926–7)*
Ambrose Palmer *(1932–8)*
Tommy Burns *(1941–7)*
Vic Patrick *(1941–6)*
Dave Sands *(1945–52)*
Jimmy Carruthers *(1948–54)*
Johnny Famechon *(1964–70)*
Lionel Rose *(1966–70)*
Rocky Mattioli *(1977–80)*
Jeff Fenech *(1985–93)*
Barry Michael *(1985–7)*
Lester Ellis *(1985)*
Joe Bugner *(1985–6)*
Grahame 'Spike' Cheney *(1988)*
Jeff 'Hitman' Harding *(1989–94)*
Kostya Tszyu *(1995–)*
Anthony Mundine *(2000–)*

Melbourne Cup

This is the richest racing event in Australia. The race began in 1861 when the background of immense wealth from the goldfields created the climate for a race such as this. Archer was the first horse to win the Melbourne Cup.

1930	Phar Lap	1950	Comic Court
1931	White Nose	1951	Delta
1932	Peter Pan	1952	Dalray
1933	Hallmark	1953	Wodalla
1934	Peter Pan	1954	Rising Fast
1935	Marabou	1955	Toparoa
1936	Wotan	1956	Evening Peal
1937	The Trump	1957	Straight Draw
1938	Catalogue	1958	Baystone
1939	Rivette	1959	Macdougal
1940	Old Rowley	1960	Hi Jinx
1941	Skipton	1961	Lord Fury
1942	Colonus	1962	Even Stevens
1943	Dark Felt	1963	Gatum Gatum
1944	Sirius	1964	Polo Prince
1945	Rainbird	1965	Light Fingers
1946	Russia	1966	Galilee
1947	Hiraji	1967	Red Handed
1948	Rimfire	1968	Rain Lover
1949	Foxzami	1969	Rain Lover

1970	Baghdad Note	1987	Kensei
1971	Silver Knight	1988	Empire Rose
1972	Piping Lane	1989	Tawrrific
1973	Gala Supreme	1990	Kingston Rule
1974	Think Big	1991	Let's Elope
1975	Think Big	1992	Subzero
1976	Van Der Hum	1993	Vintage Crop
1977	Gold and Black	1994	Jeune
1978	Arwon	1995	Doriemus
1979	Hyperno	1996	Saintly
1980	Beldale Ball	1997	Might And Power
1981	Just A Dash	1998	Jezabeel
1982	Gurner's Lane	1999	Rogan Josh
1983	Kiwi	2000	Brew
1984	Black Knight	2001	Ethereal
1985	What A Nuisance	2002	Media Puzzle
1986	At Talaq		

Fauna

Mammals

Australia has about 230 species of mammals and almost half are marsupials (pouched mammals). The balance consists of placental mammals (having a placenta which nourishes the embryo), and the monotremes, the lowest order of egg-laying mammals (having one opening for digestive, urinary and genital organs).

Marsupials

The **bandicoot** is a small animal resembling a native cat, but is insect-eating.

The **koala**, which is not a member of the bear family, lives in trees, drowsing during the day and becoming more active in the evening. It feeds on vast quantities of gum leaves which have a high oil content, enabling it to go for long periods without water. Its pouch opens downwards.

Kangaroos are represented in Australia by three subfamilies: Hypsiprymnodontinae, the Potoroinae and the Macropodinae. Their pouch opens upwards and they have a unique continuous flow of reproduction, with one joey outside the pouch which will still suckle, one inside suckling and one embryo 'on hold'. There are 45 species in Australia.

The **marsupial mole** is a small animal which lives in desert regions. It is eyeless and has no claws, unlike the true mole. It is rarely found because it lives underground.

The **numbat** is a unique striped marsupial now found only in the south-west corner of Western Australia. It is an endangered species because it is hunted by feral animals. It has sharp front claws and a sticky tongue with which it attacks ant and termite nests. Strangely, it has no pouch, the young cling with their mouths to the mother's underside until old enough to fend for themselves.

Possums are herbivorous marsupials which live in trees. They belong to four main families: ringtails and large gliders; brushtails and cuscus; feathertail and pygmy possums; and honey possums.

The **Tasmanian devil** is the largest surviving carnivorous marsupial. It is nocturnal and very shy. It is the size of a fox terrier but has strength enough in its teeth to consume a whole sheep, including the skull. The litter can remain in the pouch for months.

Also known as thylacine, the **Tasmanian tiger** is the largest carnivorous marsupial in the world. It is presumed extinct although there have been many unconfirmed sightings.

The **wombat** is a powerful, thickset, burrowing marsupial found only in Australia. Not a very sociable animal, it has a bony plate in its rump which can be used to kill any predator which might follow it into its burrow.

Placental mammals

In Australia, placental mammals (which produce fully developed young) comprise bats, dingoes, rodents and marine mammals.

The **bat** is the only true flying mammal. There are 58 species in Australia including the fruit bat and the rare ghost bat.

The **dingo** is a dog considered indigenous to Australia. It is presumed to have evolved from dogs brought from Asia 3000 to 8000 years ago by the ancestors of the Australian Aborigines. Dingoes are stealthy nocturnal hunters and often set up a continual chorus of howls much like the wolf.

Sea lions and **seals** are marine mammals found on Australia's southern coastline. **Dugongs** are herbivorous marine mammals which feed on sea grasses.

Monotremes

The **echidna** has sharp claws and a long sticky ribbon-like tongue with which it gathers up ants and termites at lightning speed. It has no teeth and relies on its stiff spines for protection. It lays a single egg which is carried and hatched in a temporary but commodious pouch formed from folds of skin.

The **platypus**, unique to Australia, is the only other egg-laying mammal in the world. It has been considered a living fossil and may be the missing link between reptiles and mammals. Its fur and tail are beaver-like, and it has webbed clawed feet and a duck-like bill which is fleshy and sensitive. The platypus lays eggs and suckles its young.

Reptiles and amphibians

Australia has about 140 species of snake, 360 species of lizard, 2 species of crocodile, 15 species of freshwater tortoise and 6 species of marine turtle.

Crocodiles

The freshwater crocodile is not dangerous to people but the saltwater species, which can grow to 7 metres long, is very dangerous. Both species are found in northern waters.

Frogs

There are approximately 130 species of frog in Australia but no salamanders. Australia's native frogs include a diverse array of tree frogs, marsh frogs and burrowing frogs.

Lizards

Australian lizards range in length from 55 mm to 2.4 metres. The great perentie or goanna is the second-largest lizard in the world. The most popular lizard is the frill-necked lizard which has a vivid frill of skin. Under attack it unfolds the frill, sways to and fro, opens its mouth wide and hisses. The blue-tongued lizard belongs to the skink family, the most prevalent lizard species in Australia.

Snakes

Of the 140 species of snake found in Australia, approximately 100 are venomous. The nonvenomous snakes include pythons, blind snakes, file snakes and some colubrid snakes. Among the venomous snakes are the death adder, the tiger snake and the taipan.

Insects

Australia has over 50 000 species of insects. There are about 350 species of butterflies, 7600 species of moths,

18 000 species of beetles and 900 species of ants. There are over 200 species of cicadas.

Arachnids

The funnel-web spider is the most poisonous spider in Australia and the male is five times more toxic than the female. The male red-back spider is one-third the size of the female and is reputed to be nonvenomous. The female is highly venomous.

Marine organisms

The Great Barrier Reef is the earth's largest structure created by living creatures. It is a complex ecological maze of fortress-like structures composed of dead coral over which the living coral forms a mantle. The living coral is made up of millions of polyps. These tiny marine animals grow and reproduce on the remains of their ancestors.

Blue-ringed octopus

These small octopuses are found over vast areas. They often take the colour of their background but when irritated light up electric-blue rings around their body. Normally they are not aggressive but can sting when disturbed and their sting can be fatal.

Crown-of-thorns starfish

This starfish is approximately 30 cm in diameter. It is not deadly but because its spines are quite toxic it is hard to handle.

Sea wasp

This creature is often referred to as the box jellyfish because of its cubic shape. It has a simple branched tentacle flowing from each corner of the cube which is extremely dangerous. It is considered to be the most poisonous creature in our seas, a sting causing death within minutes.

Birds

There are over 700 different kinds of birds in Australia including bower-builders, lyrebirds, magpies, butcherbirds and song larks.

Bellbird

They have a melodic bell-like note and are found in open forest and sheltered dells on the eastern coast.

Black swan

The black swan is unique to Australia and the only species of swan on the continent.

Bowerbird

The satin bowerbird is found only in Australia and New Guinea.

Brolga

This is the only Australian crane. It is a swamp dweller found mostly on the inland plains.

Emu

The emu is the unofficial emblem of Australia. It is flightless and stands about 1.5 metres high. It is closely related to the cassowary and next in size to the ostrich.

Honeyeater

The helmeted honeyeater is one of the rarest birds in the world. It is only found in southern Victoria, east of Port Phillip Bay.

Kookaburra

Unique to Australia; these birds are the largest of the kingfishers. There are two types, the laughing jackass of the eastern states and the blue-winged kookaburra of the north and north-west.

Lyrebird

Male lyrebirds have a fancy gauze-like tail, giving this unique bird its name. Lyrebirds are ground feeders and build incubation mounds for nests. They have a wide vocal range and are splendid mimics.

Parrots

There are more than 50 species of Australian parrots. Among them are galahs, sulphur-crested cockatoos, rosellas, lorikeets and budgerigars.

Penguin

The only penguin species residing in Australian waters is the fairy or little penguin. Phillip Island in Victoria is the home of the best-known colony.

Swift and swallow

The migratory spine-tailed swift is known as the storm bird, because it is often seen before and after a storm, feeding on the insects trapped in the air currents. The welcome swallow spends long hours soaring. These birds can feed their young without alighting on the nest.

Wedge-tailed eagle

With an average wingspan of 2.1 metres, this is Australia's largest raptor. It is found throughout Australia but is more common in the arid centre.

Flora

Although Australia is predominantly arid, with vast desert areas, there are many other vegetation regions such as rainforests, savanna grasslands, scrub, mallee, heath and alpine areas.

Australian plants in general are characterised by their drought-resistant qualities – tough spiny leaves and thick bark to resist evaporation. They are also very fire-resistant and many of these plants need a fierce fire to germinate seeds and rejuvenate.

The Australian land flora comprises over 12 000 species of flowering plants and is dominated by the eucalyptus (over 550 recognised species), paperbark, tea tree, banksia, wattle, casuarina and blackboy (grass tree).

Forests

On the northern and eastern coastlines of the Australian continent are vast areas of forest which experience rainfall ranging from 1000 to 2500 mm per year. The broadleaved rainforests of the north are dominated by buttressing fig trees, interlacing lianas, cabbage fan palms and fungi, producing a dark and brooding atmosphere.

The open forests around the top end of the Northern Territory and on the east coast are less formidable and dense. Eucalypts such as mountain ash, spotted gum and hoop pine dominate the landscape.

Grasses and woodlands

These areas of Australia are to be found mainly 200 to 300 km inland from the north and east coasts. Compared with the forest there is a greater distance between the trees and tree crowns are quite large. Here the eucalypt abounds.

Scrub and mallee

This is a diverse community of shrubby plants where the most dominant, the mallee eucalyptus, is not more than 8 metres high. It is restricted to the south-eastern and south-western regions of the country where many Australian wildflowers grow.

Deserts

The true desert prevails over vast regions of the inland. The land receives unpredictable and extremely low rainfall, temperatures are extreme, and evaporation exceeds precipitation. These adverse conditions not only create a variety of dry salt lakes and dry riverbeds but produce a complex mosaic of plant communities. Plants adapt by growing spindly leaves and tough bark to prevent evaporation.

Acknowledgements

When preparing a book such as this, there is always a considerable number of people who help with advice and information, and I sincerely thank them all. In particular, I would like to thank the staff of the following organisations: Australian Ballet; Opera Australia; Australian National Library; Mitchell Library; Department of Aboriginal Affairs; Department of the Prime Minister and Cabinet; Parliament House Education Resource, ACT; and the Premier's Department in each state.

I am also indebted to the following people for detailed information in specialised areas: Russell Best (flora and fauna); Kate Reynolds (ballet); Claire Vince (opera); Pat Yardley (art); Mark Hughes (rock music); Ross Dundas (cricket); Des Renford (swimming); and Pat Conlan (films).

List of Sources

Most of the information for this book has been adapted from the author's *The Little Aussie Fact Book* (also published by Penguin Books Australia), a larger, more detailed look at Australian facts and figures.

The author acknowledges indebtedness to the following books, which were consulted for reference:

Adams, K. M. *Australia: Colonies to the Commonwealth 1850–1900.* Angus & Robertson, 1990.

Aitken, Don and Jinks, Brian. *Australian Political Institutions.* Pitman, 1985.

Australian Museum. *The Complete Book of Australian Mammals.* Angus & Robertson, 1990.

Blanch, John. *Ampol Australian Sporting Records.* John Pollard, 1987.

Cayley, N. W. *What Bird is That?* Angus & Robertson, 1995.

Cheers, Gordon, et al. *Australia Through Time*. Random House, 1998.

—— *Australian Sport Through Time*. Random House, 1997.

Cronin, L. *Key Guide to Australian Trees*. Reed, 1997.

—— *Key Guide to Australian Wildflowers*. Reed, 1995.

Draper, W. J. (ed.). *Who's Who in Australia*. Herald & Weekly Times, 1984.

Fraser, Bryce (ed.). *The Macquarie Book of Events*. Macquarie Library, 1990.

Gleeson, James. *Australian Painters*. Lansdowne, 1989.

Shaw, John. *Australian Encyclopaedia*. Collins, 1984.

Simpson, Ken, Day, Nicolas, and Trusler, Peter. *Field Guide to the Birds of Australia*. Viking, 1999.

Stratton, David. *The Avocado Plantation*. Pan Macmillan, 1990.

United Nations. *Demographic Yearbook*. 1998.

Facts and figures on demographics and the economy are from the Australian Bureau of Statistics and the Australian Stock Exchange.